Dedicated to:

The students of M.J. Fletcher Elementary School.

About

This coloring book includes artwork created by the 4th grade students of
Milton J. Fletcher Elementary School in Jamestown, N.Y.
All proceeds from the sale of this book go directly to the school.
Also evident in the book are the Positive Behavioral Interventions and Supports
(PBIS) school-wide expectations:

Be Respectful
Be Responsible
Be Safe

Student artwork by:
Veronica Short
Brynn Ribbing
Gabriella Knight
Cordell Simmons
Luis Diaz
Ella Attaway
Keyamari Keys
Peyton Joly
Zoe Alianell
Warrick Darling

Additional Artwork by:
Darryl Mallanda

Cover Artwork by:
Darryl Mallanda

2017-2018

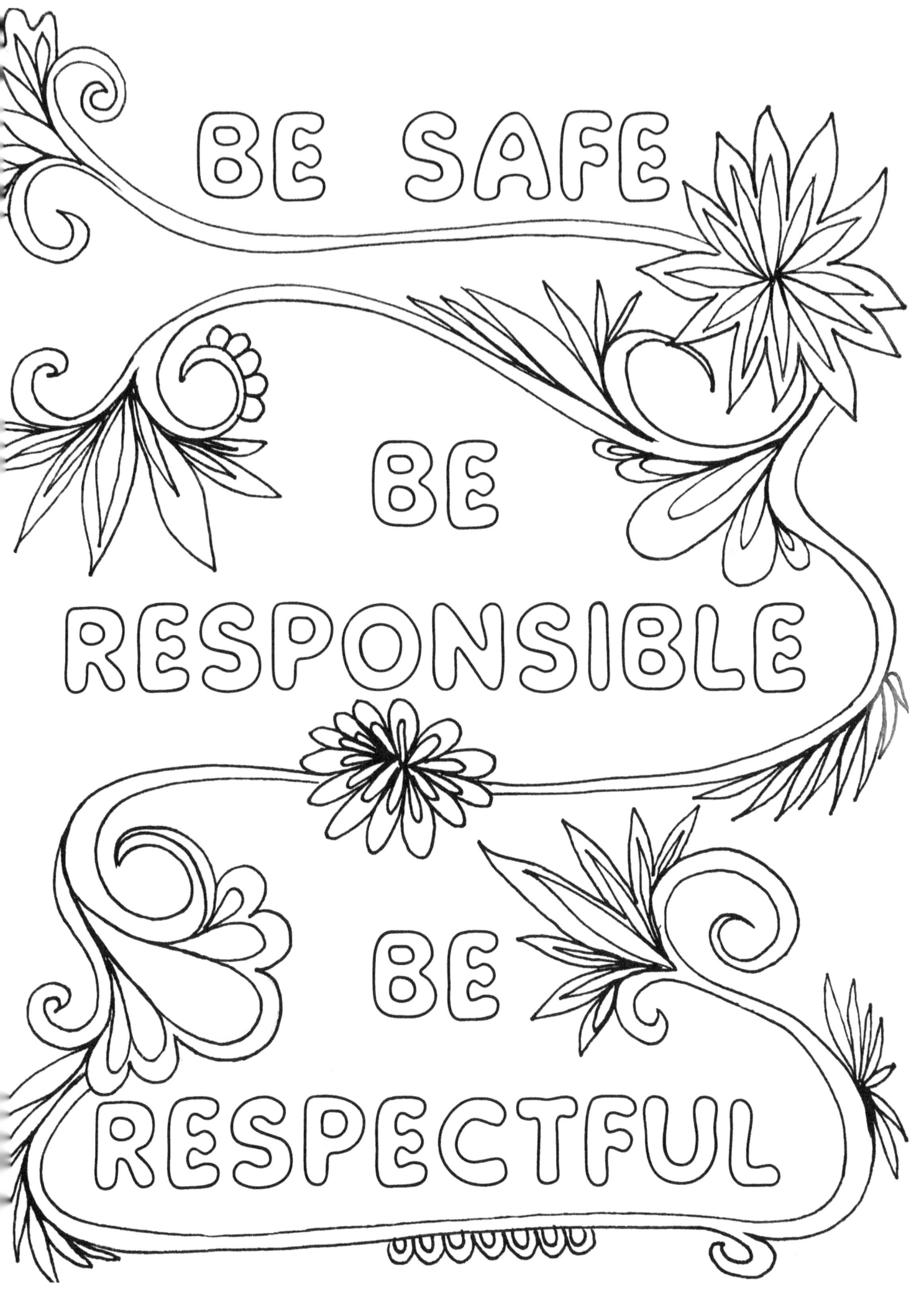

FLETCHER ELEMENTARY

BE GREAT

Reading is fun!

Yay

The Notebook	Justice
Brave	The little dog
Cat	art
gym	Love

M.J. Fletcher School!!

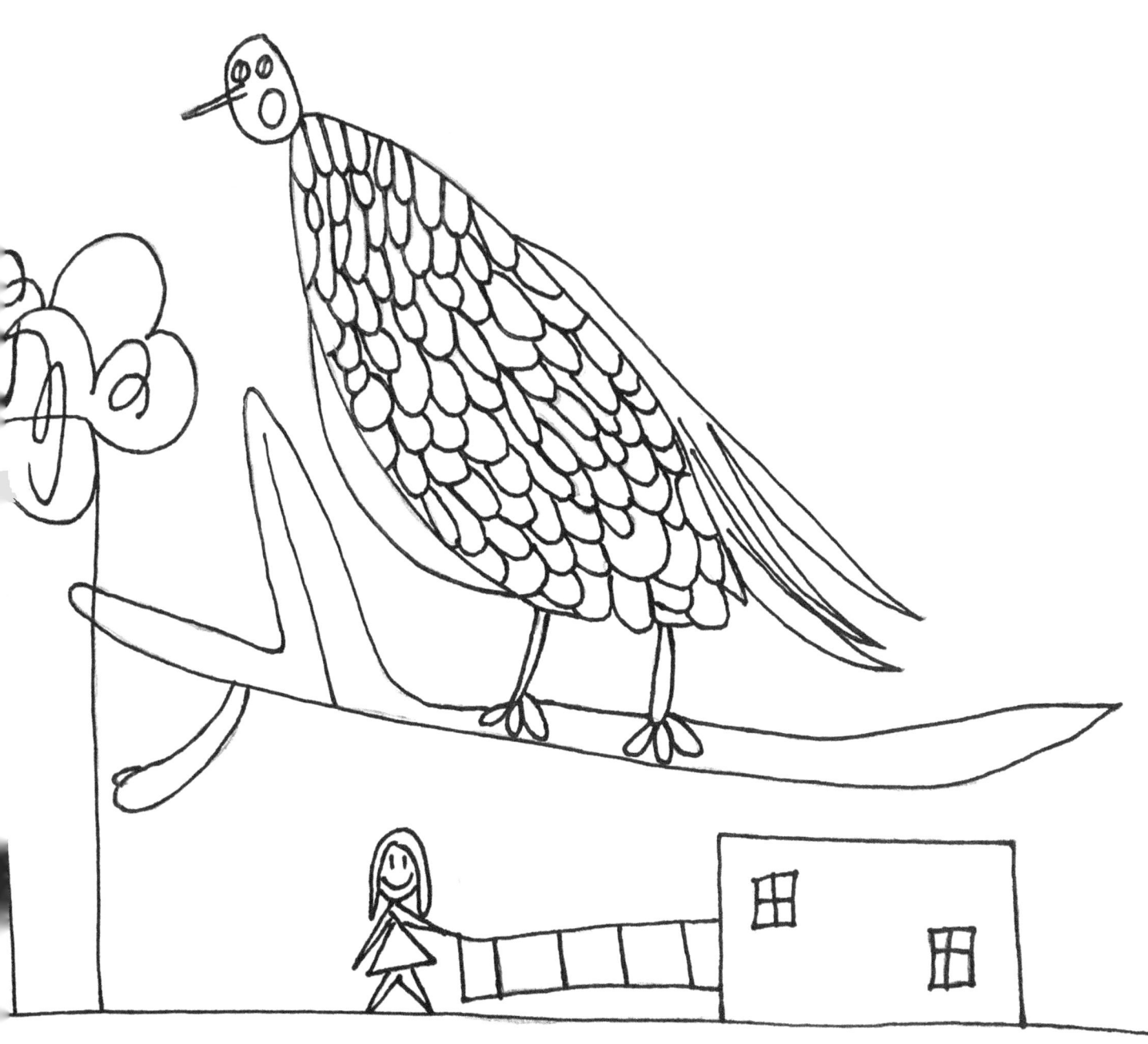

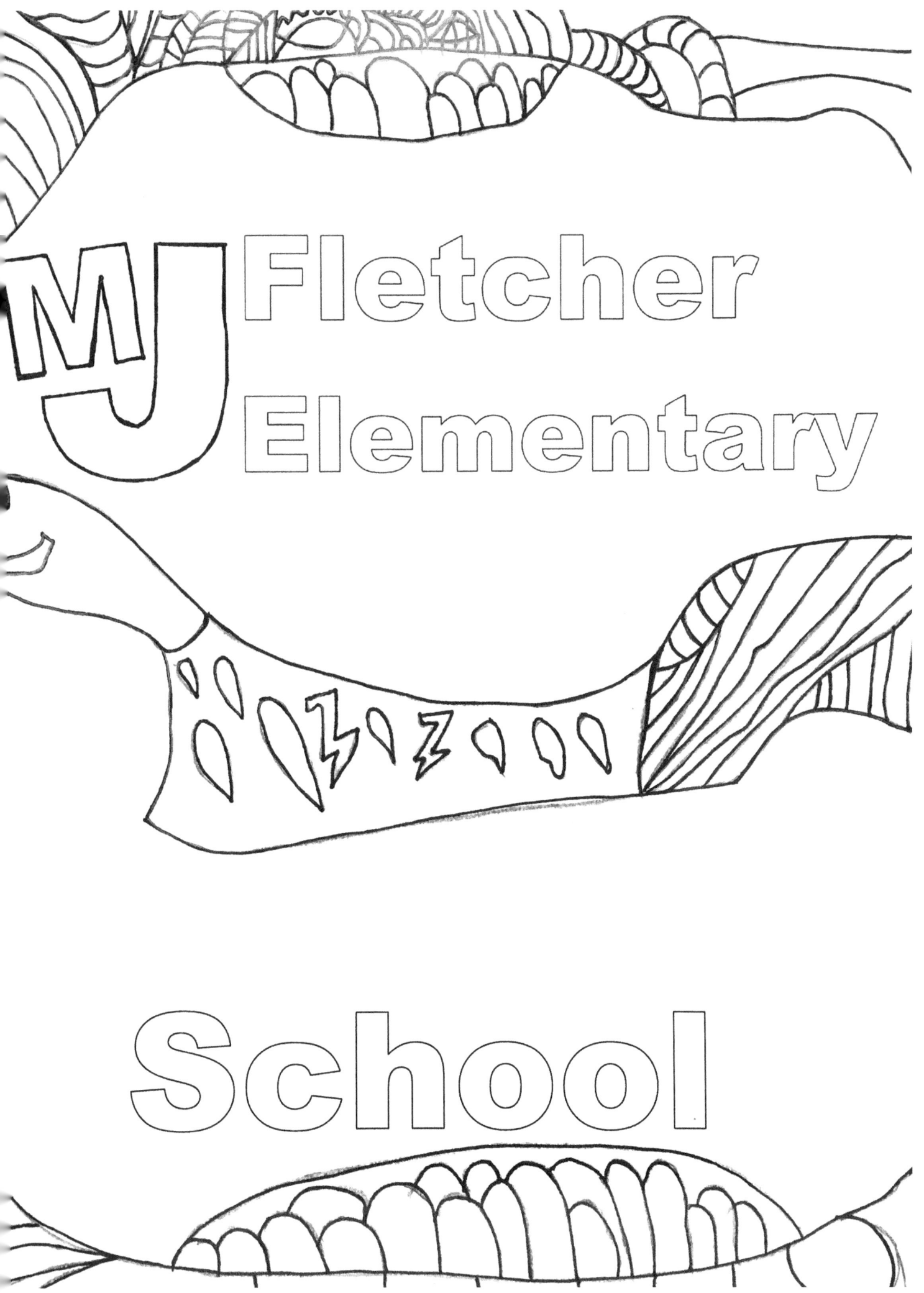

I don't know but I've been told.
Fletcher's kids are good as gold.
They know how to act in school.
Good behavior is really cool!

Be Safe!

Be Respectful!

Be Responsible!

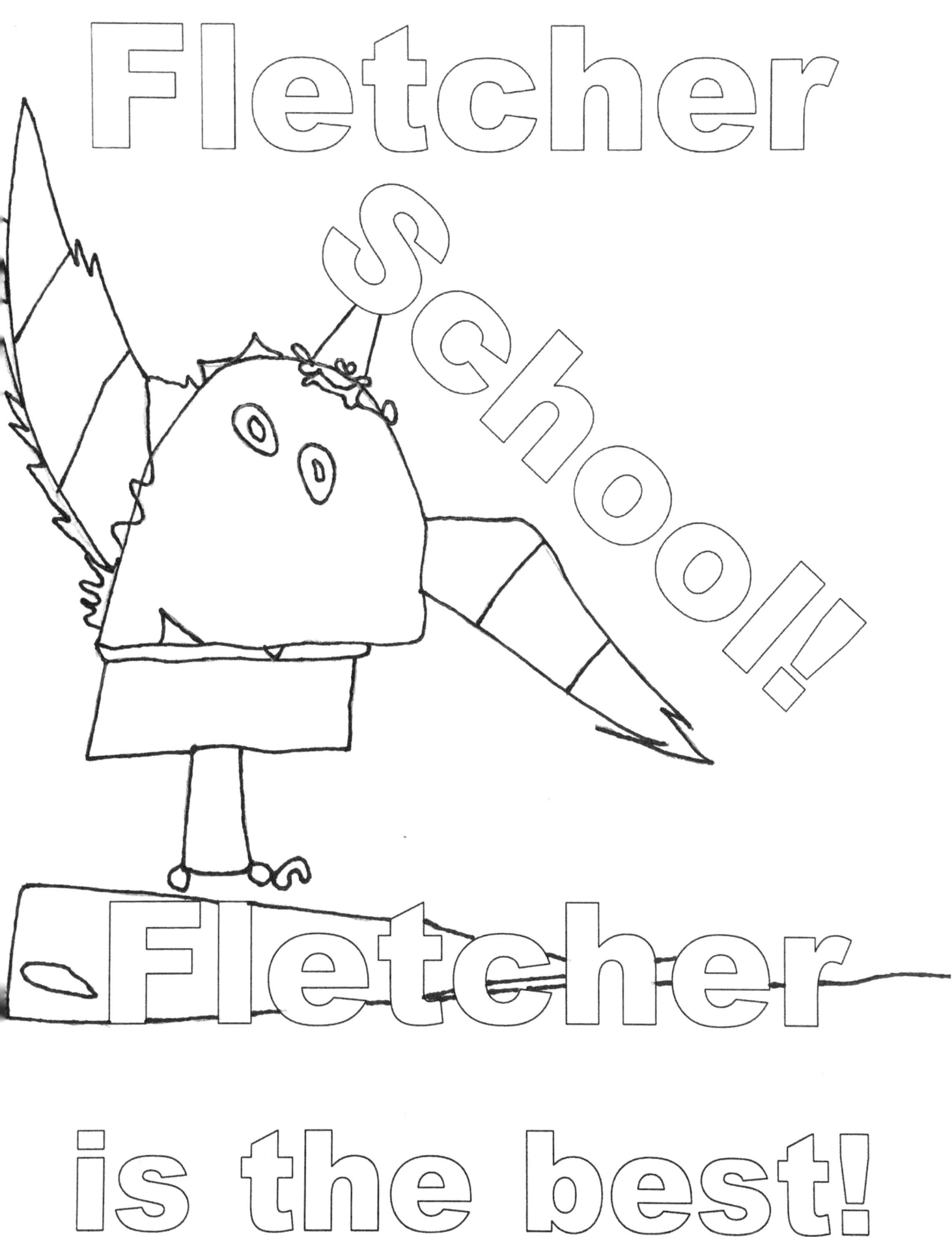

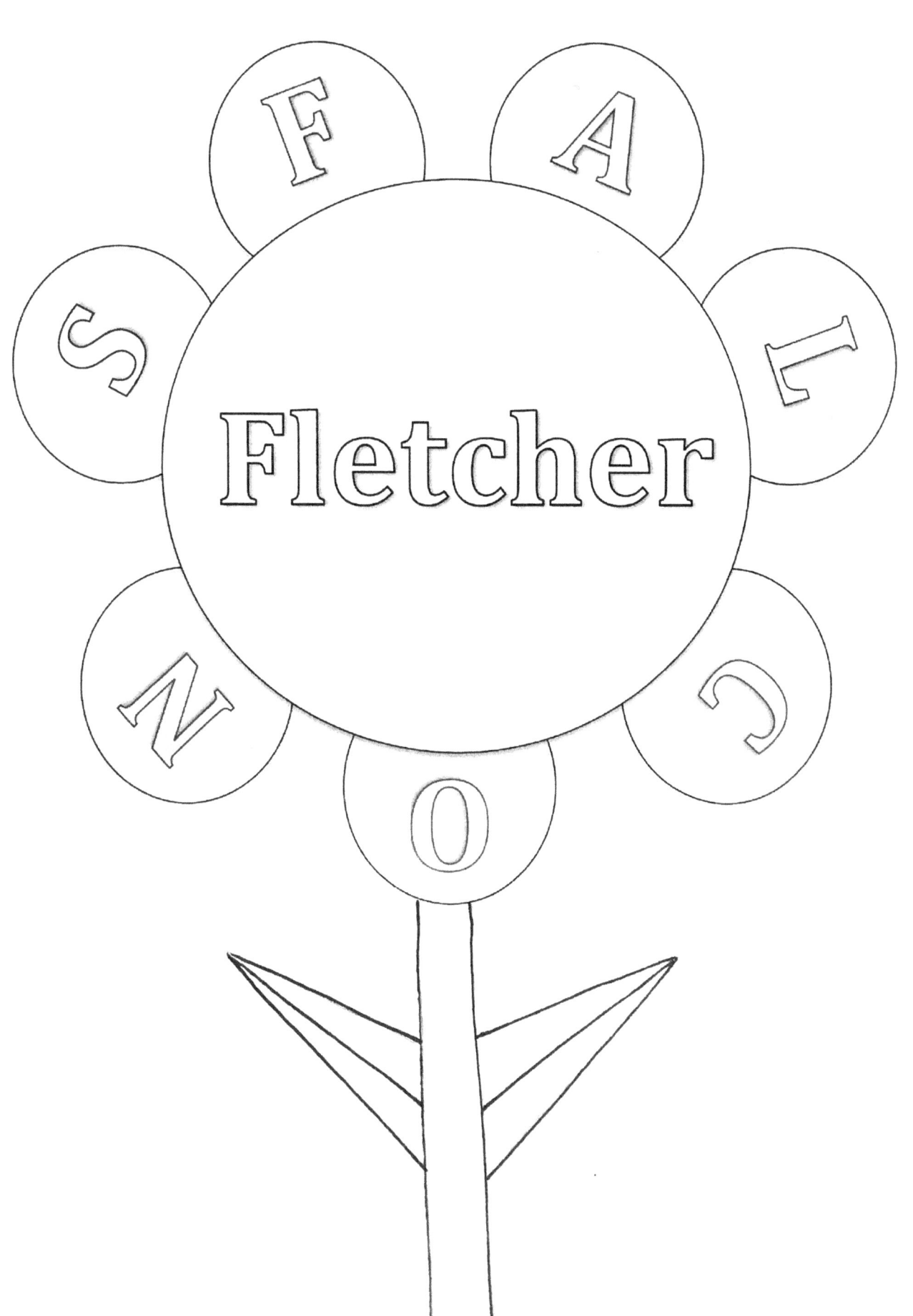

M.J. FLETCHER SCHOOL FALCONS

Be safe

Be responsible

Be respectful

I throw my hands up in the air sometimes
Sayin' alright! I'm gonna shine bright!
I'm workin' every day to shine my light
Sayin' alright! I'm gonna shine bright!

Cause we're gonna rock this school
We're gonna shine so bright!
We're gonna light it up
Like it's dynamite!

There's a leader in me
When I choose to act right
You just watch and see
I am dynamite!

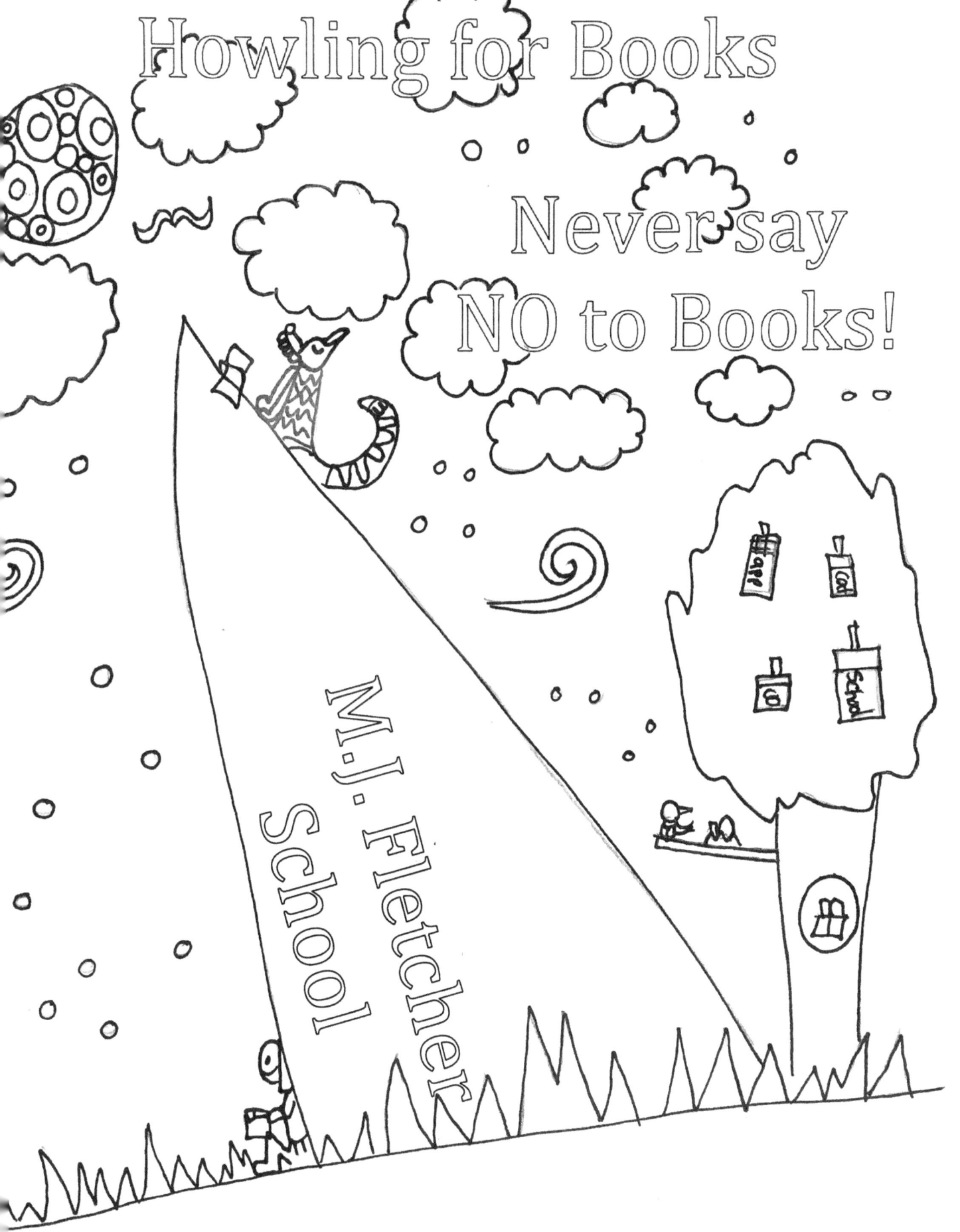

M. J. Fletcher Elementary School

Be Safe
Be Respectful
Be Responsible

www.ingramcontent.com/pod-product-compliance
Lightning Source LLC
Chambersburg PA
CBHW062237220526
45471CB00009B/3522